A Comparison of Official Poverty Estimates in the Redesigned Current Population Survey Annual Social and Economic Supplement

Joshua Mitchell[1]

U.S. Census Bureau

Trudi Renwick

U.S. Census Bureau

January 4, 2015

SEHSD Working Paper #2014-35

Abstract

This paper presents a descriptive analysis of the poverty estimates from the 2014 Current Population Survey Annual Social and Economic Supplement (CPS ASEC) redesigned and traditional survey questionnaires. The 2014 CPS ASEC utilized a probability split panel design to test a new redesigned set of income questions. The income questions were redesigned with the goals of improving income reporting, increasing response rates, reducing reporting errors by taking better advantage of an automated questionnaire environment, and updating questions on retirement income and the income generated from retirement accounts and all other assets. Our main finding is that, among the demographic subgroups examined, most differences between the poverty estimates for the samples assigned to the traditional and redesigned survey instruments were not statistically significant but child (people under age 18) and elderly (people age 65 and older) poverty were higher in the sample assigned to the redesigned questionnaire despite the higher aggregate, mean, and median income collected in the sample with the redesigned questions compared to the sample with the traditional questions.

---

[1] Joshua Mitchell and Trudi Renwick are economists with the Social, Economic and Housing Statistics Division of the U.S. Census Bureau, 4600 Silver Hill Road, Washington, DC 20233 (joshua.w mitchell@census.gov trudi.j.renwick@census.gov). Paper presented at the January 2015 Allied Social Sciences Association, Boston, Massachusetts. This paper reports the results of research and analysis undertaken by Census Bureau staff. Any views expressed are those of the authors and not necessarily those of the U.S. Census Bureau.

Introduction

This paper presents a descriptive analysis of the poverty estimates from the 2014 CPS ASEC redesigned and traditional survey instruments. The 2014 CPS ASEC utilized a probability split panel design to test a redesigned set of income questions. There were approximately 98,000 addresses in the 2014 CPS ASEC sample; a subsample of about 30,000 addresses was randomly assigned to be eligible to receive what we refer to as the "redesigned" income questions, the remaining sample (approximately 68,000 addresses) was eligible to receive the set of ASEC income questions that has been in use since 1994, referred to here as the "traditional" income questions. The source of data for the Income and Poverty in the United States: 2013 report was the portion of the sample that received the traditional income questions.

The income questions were redesigned with the goals of improving income reporting, increasing response rates, reducing reporting errors by taking better advantage of an automated questionnaire environment, and updating questions on retirement income and the income generated from retirement accounts and all other assets. The following were components of the redesigned instrument:

- Tailoring the order of income questions to match those sources most likely received by respondents given certain known characteristics of the respondent focusing on households with a householder aged 62 and older, lower income households, and a default for all other household types.

- Using a dual-pass identifying all sources of income received first and then asking amounts for those sources the respondent indicated receiving.

- Using income ranges as a follow-up for "don't know" or "refused" income amount questions.

- Removing the family income screener for determining which households to ask low-income sources (such as Temporary Assistance for Needy Families [TANF]).

- Changing the disability questions to eliminate confusion between disability from Social Security and Supplemental Security Income (SSI).

- Collecting lump sum back-payments for disability benefits.

- Using a new strategy to collect property income by asking separately about income from retirement accounts and other assets.

- Collecting the value of assets that generate income if the respondent is unsure of the income generated.

- Asking about retirement account withdrawals and distributions.

Our goal is to better understand how the redesigned income questions affect poverty estimates by comparing the estimates from the sample of individuals who received the redesigned income questions to the estimates from the sample that received the traditional income questions.

Our main finding is that, among the demographic subgroups examined, most differences between the two samples are not statistically significant. We do find that the number of people in poverty and the poverty rate are higher for children, the elderly, and Asians in the sample selected to receive the redesigned questions. There are more families with a female householder in poverty in the sample with the redesigned income questions, but the difference in the poverty rate of these families is not statistically significant. In contrast, the number of people in poverty is lower in the sample selected to receive the redesigned questions for people with a disability, people who worked and for those who work less than full-time year-round. The poverty rate is lower for all workers and those who worked less than full-time year-round. [2]

As demonstrated in Semega et al. (2015), the redesigned income questions do succeed in collecting considerably more aggregate, mean, and median income; however, these poverty estimates hint that this increase in income does not extend to the lowest percentiles of the income distribution. There is, therefore, no evidence that the redesigned income questions reduce the measured poverty rate in 2013.

The paper first examines changes in the poverty rates across the two samples. Next the paper looks at differences in two measures of the depth of poverty. The third section of the paper provides an analysis of the differences in poverty estimates across the two samples, focusing on the two demographic groups whose poverty rates were greater in the sample with the redesigned income questions than in the sample with the traditional income questions. The final section of the paper looks at some alternative indicators of socio-economic status to assess whether the differences in the sample composition rather than differences in the questionnaires.

---

[2] The estimates in this paper are from the 2014 Annual Social and Economic Supplement (ASEC) to the Current Population Survey (CPS). The estimates in this paper (which may be shown in text, figures, and tables) are based on responses from a sample of the population and may differ from actual values because of sampling variability or other factors. As a result, apparent differences between the estimates for two or more groups may not be statistically significant. All comparative statements have undergone statistical testing and are significant at the 90 percent confidence level unless otherwise noted. Standard errors were calculated using replicate weights. Further information about the source and accuracy of the estimates is available at < ftp://ftp2.census.gov/programs-surveys/cps/techdocs/cpsmar14.pdf>.

Poverty Comparison

As shown in Table 1, the overall poverty rate in 2013 was 14.7 percent (46 million people) for the sample assigned to the redesigned instrument compared to the official poverty rate of 14.5 percent (45 million people) for the sample with the traditional instrument. Neither the number of people in poverty nor the poverty rate was statistically different across the two samples. We next explore poverty estimates across demographic subgroups.

Age

- The child poverty rate was 21.3 percent (16 million people) for sample with redesigned instrument—this was 1.4 percentage points higher (1 million more children) than the rate for the sample with the traditional instrument.
- The poverty rate for adults age 18 to 64 was 13.3 percent (26 million people) for the sample with the redesigned questions, not statistically different from the sample with the traditional questions.
- The poverty rate for the elderly was 10.3 percent (5 million people)—0.8 percentage points higher (400,000 more elderly) for the sample with the redesigned questions than the sample with the traditional questions.

Sex

- Differences in poverty rates by sex were not statistically significant across samples.

Race and Hispanic Origin

- For Asians, the poverty rate was 13.0 percent (2.2 million people) for the sample with the redesigned survey instrument. This was 2.5 percentage points higher than the poverty rate for Asians for the sample with the traditional instrument.
- Differences in the poverty rates for other race and ethnic groups were not statistically significant across the two samples.

Families

- The estimate of the number of female householders in poverty from the sample with the redesigned questions was 5 million, a half a million more than the estimate from the sample with the traditional questions. The difference in the poverty rate for female householders was not statistically significant across the two samples.

Nativity

- Differences in poverty rates by nativity were not statistically significant across the two samples.

Region

- Differences in regional poverty rates were not statistically significant between the two samples.

Residence

- Differences in poverty rates by residence (inside metropolitan statistical areas vs. outside metropolitan statistical areas) between the two samples were not statistically significant.

Work Experience

- Poverty rates for all workers and workers who worked less than full-time, year-round were lower for the sample with the redesigned questions than the poverty rates for these groups for the sample with the traditional questions.

Disability

- There were 350 thousand fewer disabled people in poverty in the sample with the redesigned instrument but the difference in poverty rates between the two samples was not statistically significant.

Depth of Poverty

While the poverty rate shows the proportion of people with income below the relevant poverty threshold, additional insight can be gained by examining the depth of poverty. The income-to-poverty ratio shows how close a family's income is to its poverty threshold. The income deficit or surplus shows how many dollars a family's or an individual's income is below (or above) the poverty threshold.

Table 2 shows income-to-poverty ratios for the two samples. For the total population there are no differences between the two samples in the number and share of people below 50, 125, 150 and 200 percent of the poverty line. As discussed earlier, the number and share of children in poverty is higher in the sample with the redesigned income questions and this also holds for the under 50% income-to-poverty threshold category.

Table 3 shows income deficits and surpluses in the two samples. Among families and unrelated individuals, there are no significant differences in average and median deficits between the two samples. In contrast, across all families, married couples, female householders, and unrelated individuals, there are higher average and median surpluses in the sample with the redesigned questions. Overall, the average surplus is $78,468 in the sample with the redesigned questions and $74,667 in the sample with the traditional questions while the median surplus is $53,695 and $51,839 respectively. The larger surpluses in the sample with the redesigned questions reflect the greater amount of income collected in the upper part of the income distribution.

Analysis

Since the redesigned income questions collected more aggregate, mean and median income, one might expect to see lower poverty rates for the sample with the redesigned questions. Given the higher rates of child and elderly poverty found in the sample with the redesigned questions, we seek to explain the sources of these differences both within and between demographic subgroups. Rather than describe results in depth for all demographic subgroups, we focus on those that are statistically different across the two samples.

Demographic Composition Comparison

The Census Bureau weights each record in a sample to provide estimates that are nationally representatives. There are several stages to this weighting procedure, designed to control for race, age, sex, ethnicity and state of residence.[3] However, there are other demographic characteristics that are not targeted in the weighting. A comparison of the demographic composition of the samples assigned to the redesigned and traditional questionnaires is shown in Table 4. After weighting, there were still several statistically significant differences in the composition of the two samples:

- The number of elderly was 455,000 thousand higher in the sample with the redesigned questions. The share of the elderly in this sample was 0.1 percent higher than in the sample with the traditional questions.

- There were 117 thousand fewer Blacks in the sample with the redesigned questions than in the sample with the traditional questions, however, the Black shares of the two samples were not statistically different.

- There were 1.1 million more householders in the sample with the redesigned questions. The share of people who were householders was .3 percentage points higher in the sample with the redesigned questions.

- People in female householders with no husband present made up 16.0 percent of the sample with the redesigned questions, 0.9 percent more than they did in the sample with the traditional questions. There were 3 million more people living in families with female householders in the sample with the redesigned questions.

Children

Table 5 shows the demographic composition of the children from the two samples. There were no differences in sample composition found across race, region or residence groups.[4]

- We find that 26.0 percent of children (19 million) in the sample with the redesigned questions were from families with a female householder and no husband present compared to only 24.8 percent (18 million people) in the sample with the traditional questions.

---

[3] For more information about how the Census Bureau applies weights to each record, see Technical Paper 66, Design and Methodology at http://www.census.gov/prod/2006pubs/tp-66.pdf.
[4] While the difference in the share of female vs. male children across the two samples was not statistically significant, there were 251,000 fewer female children in the sample with the redesigned income questions.

- This difference in children in female-householder families was offset by a lower rate of children in married-couple families, 65.7 percent (48 million people) in the sample with the redesigned questions versus 67.2 percent (49 million people) in the other sample.

Since children in female householder families have higher poverty rates than those in married-couple families, the difference in family composition can help explain the overall difference in child poverty rates.

If the percent of children living in families with female householders were the same in the sample with the redesigned questions as the sample with the traditional questions, the child poverty rate for the sample with the redesigned questions would be 20.7 percent, not statistically different from the poverty rate for children from the sample with the traditional questions. (The 90 percent confidence interval for the difference in the poverty rates was 1.1 percentage points.)

	Traditional Income Questions		Redesigned Income Questions		Sample with Redesigned Income Questions with Shares from the Sample with the Traditional Income Questions	
Married Couple Families	67.2%	9.5%	65.7%	10.0%	67.2%	10.0%
Families with a Female Householder	24.8%	45.8%	26.0%	47.0%	24.8%	47.0%
Families with a Male Householder	6.9%	22.5%	6.9%	24.5%	6.9%	24.5%
In Unrelated Subfamilies	1.0%	47.7%	1.2%	48.8%	1.0%	48.8%
Unrelated Individuals	0.2%	92.8%	0.3%	92.8%	0.2%	92.8%
Poverty Rate for All Children		19.9%		21.3%		20.7%

There was also a statistically significant nativity difference—96.8 percent (71.1 million) of the children in the sample with the redesigned questions were native born compared with 96.3 percent (70.9 million people) of the children in the sample with the traditional questions.[5] This 0.5 percentage point difference is accounted for by the lower share of non-citizen children in the sample with the redesigned questions. Since the poverty rate for non-citizen children is higher than it is for natives, this demographic difference does not explain why child poverty is higher in the sample with the redesigned questions.

In addition to differences in demographic composition, there were also differences in child poverty rates within demographic subgroups as shown in Table 6. While not always statistically significant, most point estimates of child poverty were higher in the sample with the redesigned questions. The child poverty rate was higher in the sample with the redesigned questions for both sexes, natives, those living in the Midwest, those living in metropolitan statistical areas outside of principal cities and those living outside metropolitan statistical areas.

---

[5] The difference in the number of native-born children across the two samples was not statically significant.

Child poverty rate differences by race were more complex. The child poverty rate was 2.5 percentage points higher for Whites and 5.0 percentage points higher for Asians in the sample with the redesigned questions. However, the poverty rate was 4.4 percentage points *lower* for Blacks.

Examining the lower end of the income distribution, families with income below 200 percent of their poverty threshold, changes in average family income are consistent with the poverty differences. Appendix Table A compares aggregate and mean income by detailed income source for all families with children, Black families with children, non-Black families with children and Asian families with children.

The average total income and average total earnings of Black families with children were higher in the sample with the redesigned questions than in the sample with the traditional questions. On the other hand, average total income and average total earnings for non-Black families with children below 200 percent of the poverty threshold were lower in the sample with the redesigned questions.

There is some evidence that these differences in earnings are driven by differences in the number of hours worked, not the redesign of the questionnaire. The average number of total hours worked for non-Black families with children below 200 percent of poverty decreased from 2,395 hours per year in the sample with the traditional questions to 2,308 in the sample with the redesigned questions. For Black families with children the difference in the hours worked was not statistically significant.

The sample size for Asian families with children is quite small, particularly for the sample with the redesigned income questions. For this group the only statistically significant changes were a decrease in average Social Security benefits, an increase in average SSI benefits and a decrease in Survivor's Income. The changes in hours worked, total income and total earnings were not significant for this group.

Elderly

Table 7 shows the demographic composition of the elderly in the two samples. Recall that there are a half-million more elderly in the sample with the redesigned questions.

- White elderly compose 0.4 percent more (600,000 more people) in the sample with the redesigned questions than the sample with the traditional questions.
- Black elderly compose 0.2 percent less (42,000) of the sample with the redesigned questions.[6]
- Men make up 0.6 percent more (500,000 people) of the elderly in the sample with the redesigned questions.

---

[6] The difference in the number of Black elderly across the two samples was not statistically significant.

- There is also one geographic difference: there are 1.2 percentage points fewer (400,000 people) elderly in the West in the sample with the redesigned questions.

Overall, these differences in demographic composition do not appear to help explain the higher elderly poverty rate in the sample with the redesigned questions.

Table 8 displays elderly poverty rates for demographic subgroups. The higher poverty rate in the sample with the redesigned questions is driven by the higher poverty rate of unrelated individuals (both men and women) where the rate is 3 percentage points higher (460,000 more people).

One geographic difference is also apparent--the poverty rate for the elderly is 2.2 percent higher (160,000 more people) in the West in the sample with the redesigned questions.[7]

Appendix Table B provides summary data on aggregate income, mean income and recipiency rates by source for the two groups of elderly with statistically significant increases in their poverty rates. The estimates look at the lower end of the distribution, individuals with family income below 200 percent of their poverty thresholds. The estimates in this table show that the differences in the aggregate income amounts for the specific income sources were not statistically significant.

Alternative Indicators of Socio-Economic Status

Two other indicators can help explain why there is no evidence that poverty is lower in the sample with the redesigned income questions despite the higher aggregate amounts of income collected. Table 9 compares recipiency rates for several types of means-tested benefits. Among people of all ages there are higher reported rates of receipt for SSI, Medicaid, and SNAP in the sample with the redesigned income questions. For example, 13.7 percent of this sample report receiving SNAP, while only 12.3 percent of the sample with the traditional income questions report SNAP receipt. Higher rates of SNAP were also reported for the elderly and higher rates of SSI were reported for both children and the elderly in the sample with the redesigned questions.

Table 10 shows estimates by detailed income source of the number of recipients and aggregate income amounts for people in the lowest quintile of the household income distribution. For these individuals, earnings were lower in the sample with the redesigned questions than the estimates of earnings for the sample with the traditional questions. The only two income sources with statistically significant increases in aggregate income were public assistance and disability benefits.

---

[7] The difference in the number of elderly in poverty in the West across the two samples was not statistically significant.

Conclusion

Our analysis of the CPS March ASEC shows that the redesigned income questions did not change overall poverty estimates for 2013. For children and the elderly, poverty is higher in the sample that received the redesigned questions. We can account for the elevated child poverty rate by the higher share of children living families with female householders in the sample with the redesigned questions. For the elderly, it is more challenging to account for the difference in poverty rates for the two samples. Evidence from means-tested transfer programs recipiency rates suggests that the sample selected to receive the redesigned income questions included more people with low incomes, even as more aggregate income was reported in this sample.

References

DeNavas-Walt, Carmen and Bernadette D. Proctor. 2014. "Income and Poverty in the United States: 2013." Current Population Reports P60-249. U.S. Census Bureau. September.

Semega, Jessican and Edward Welniak. "The Effect of the Changes to the Current Population Survey Annual Social and Economic Supplement on Estimates of Income", forthcoming.

U.S. Census Bureau. 2006. "Current Population Survey Design and Methodology." Technical Paper 66. U.S. Census Bureau. October.

Table 1.

People and Families in Poverty by Selected Characteristics: Redesigned Income Questions minus Traditional Income Questions - 2013

(Numbers in thousands, confidence intervals (C.I.) in thousands or percentage points as appropriate. People as of March of the following year. For information on confidentiality protection, sampling error, nonsampling error, and definitions, see ftp://ftp2.census.gov/programs-surveys/cps/techdocs/cpsmar14.pdf)

Characteristic	Traditional Income Questions					Redesigned Income Questions					Change in Poverty (Redesigned less Traditional)[2]	
	Total	Number in Poverty	90 percent C.I.[1] (+/-)	Percent in Poverty	90 percent C.I.[1] (+/-)	Total	Number in Poverty	90 percent C.I.[1] (+/-)	Percent in Poverty	90 percent C.I.[1] (+/-)	Number	Percent
PEOPLE												
Total	312,965	45,318	1,014	14.5	0.3	313,096	46,100	1,415	14.7	0.5	782	0.2
Family Status												
In families.............	254,988	31,530	845	12.4	0.3	256,070	32,511	1,331	12.7	0.5	981	0.3
Householder............	81,217	9,130	247	11.2	0.3	82,316	9,574	399	11.6	0.5	443	0.4
Related children under age 18	72,573	14,142	445	19.5	0.6	72,246	14,983	706	20.7	1.0 *	841 *	1.3
Related children under age 6	23,585	5,231	225	22.2	1.0	23,606	5,495	338	23.3	1.4	264	1.1
In unrelated subfamilies.	1,413	608	114	43.0	6.3	1,626	720	211	44.3	8.3	112	1.3
Reference person........	595	246	48	41.3	6.4	661	269	84	40.7	8.3	23	-0.6
Children under 18......	714	340	69	47.7	6.7	844	412	122	48.8	9.2	72	1.2
Unrelated individual.....	56,564	13,181	414	23.3	0.6	55,400	12,869	576	23.2	0.9	-312	-0.1
Race[3] and Hispanic Origin												
White alone..	243,085	29,936	816	12.3	0.3	243,346	30,997	1,023	12.7	0.4	1,061	0.4
White alone, not Hispanic	195,167	18,796	722	9.6	0.4	195,118	19,407	746	9.9	0.4	611	0.3
Black alone..	40,615	11,041	506	27.2	1.3	40,498	10,362	638	25.6	1.6	-679	-1.6
Asian alone..	17,063	1,785	176	10.5	1.0	17,257	2,248	331	13.0	1.9 *	463 *	2.6
Hispanic (of any race)	54,145	12,744	513	23.5	0.9	54,181	13,218	811	24.4	1.5	474	0.9
Sex												
Male..	153,361	20,119	568	13.1	0.4	153,465	20,138	726	13.1	0.5	19	0.0
Female..	159,605	25,199	573	15.8	0.4	159,630	25,962	877	16.3	0.6	763	0.5
Age												
Under age 18	73,625	14,659	455	19.9	0.6	73,439	15,633	709	21.3	1.0 *	974 *	1.4
Aged 18 to 64	194,833	26,429	648	13.6	0.3	194,694	25,837	874	13.3	0.4	-592	-0.3
Aged 65 and over	44,508	4,231	227	9.5	0.5	44,963	4,631	267	10.3	0.6 *	400 *	0.8
Nativity												
Native..........	271,968	37,921	943	13.9	0.3	272,423	38,702	1,257	14.2	0.5	781	0.3
Foreign born..	40,997	7,397	373	18.0	0.8	40,673	7,399	559	18.2	1.2	1	0.1
Naturalized citizen....	19,147	2,425	173	12.7	0.9	19,247	2,144	245	11.1	1.2	-281	-1.5
Not a citizen..	21,850	4,972	311	22.8	1.2	21,426	5,254	507	24.5	1.9	282	1.8
Region												
Northeast...........	55,478	7,046	437	12.7	0.8	55,529	7,218	665	13.0	1.2	173	0.3
Midwest...............	66,785	8,590	430	12.9	0.7	66,732	9,070	613	13.6	0.9	480	0.7
South..	116,961	18,870	706	16.1	0.6	116,956	19,104	953	16.3	0.8	234	0.2
West..............	73,742	10,812	434	14.7	0.6	73,879	10,708	639	14.5	0.9	-105	-0.2

Table 1.

People and Families in Poverty by Selected Characteristics: Redesigned Income Questions minus Traditional Income Questions - 2013

(Numbers in thousands, confidence intervals (C.I.) in percentages or percentage points as appropriate. People as of March of the following year. For information on confidentiality protection, sampling error, nonsampling error, and definitions, see ftp://ftp2.census.gov/programs-surveys/cps/techdocs/cpsmar14.pdf)

Characteristic	Total	Traditional Income Questions			Total	Redesigned Income Questions			Change in Poverty (Redesigned less Traditional)[2]	
		Number in Poverty	Percent in Poverty	90 percent C.I.[1] (+/-)		Number in Poverty	Percent in Poverty	90 percent C.I.[1] (+/-)	Number	Percent
Residence										
Inside metropolitan statistical areas	265,915	37,746	14.2	0.4	265,301	37,911	14.3	0.5	165	0.1
Inside principal cities	102,149	19,530	19.1	0.7	101,094	18,620	18.4	1.0	-910	-0.7
Outside principal cities	163,767	18,217	11.1	0.4	164,207	19,291	11.7	0.6	1,074	0.6
Outside metropolitan statistical areas[4]	47,050	7,572	16.1	1.0	47,795	8,190	17.1	1.3	617	1.0
Work Experience										
Total, aged 18 to 64	194,833	26,429	13.6	0.3	194,694	25,837	13.3	0.4	-592	-0.3
All workers (aged 18 to 64)	146,252	10,736	7.3	0.2	146,859	10,168	6.9	0.3 *	-568 *	-0.4
Worked full-time year-round	100,855	2,771	2.7	0.2	101,179	3,016	3.0	0.2	245	0.2
Not full-time year-round	45,397	7,965	17.5	0.6	45,680	7,152	15.7	0.8 *	-813 *	-1.9
Did not work at least one week	48,581	15,693	32.3	0.9	47,834	15,669	32.8	1.2	-24	0.5
Disability Status[5]										
Total, aged 18 to 64	194,833	26,429	13.6	0.3	194,694	25,837	13.3	0.4	-592	-0.3
With a disability	15,098	4,352	28.8	1.2	14,461	3,997	27.6	2.0 *	-354	-1.2
Without a disability	178,761	22,023	12.3	0.3	179,206	21,730	12.1	0.4	-293	-0.2
FAMILIES										
Total	81,217	9,130	11.2	0.3	82,316	9,574	11.6	0.5	443	0.4
Married-couple	59,692	3,476	5.8	0.3	59,643	3,378	5.7	0.4	-98	-0.2
Female householder, no husband present	15,195	4,646	30.6	1.1	16,176	5,168	31.9	1.5 *	521	1.4
Male householder, no wife present	6,330	1,008	15.9	1.4	6,497	1,028	15.8	2.4	20	-0.1

*Significantly different from zero at the 90 percent confidence level.

[1] A 90 percent confidence interval is a measure of an estimate's variability. The larger the confidence interval in relation to the size of the estimate, the less reliable the estimate. Confidence intervals shown in this table are based on standard errors calculated using replicate weights instead of the generalized variance function used in the past. For more information see "Standard Errors and Their Use" at ftp://ftp2.census gov/library/publications/2014/demo/p60-249sa.pdf.

[2] Details may not sum to totals because of rounding.

[3] Federal surveys now give respondents the option of reporting more than one race. Therefore, two basic ways of defining a race group are possible. A group such as Asian may be defined as those who reported Asian and no other race (the race-alone or single-race concept) or as those who reported Asian regardless of whether they also reported another race (the race-alone-or-in-combination concept). This table shows data using the first approach (race alone). The use of the single-race population does not imply that it is the preferred method of presenting or analyzing data. The Census Bureau uses a variety of approaches. Information on people who reported more than one race, such as White *and* American Indian and Alaska Native or Asian *and* Black or African American, is available from Census 2010 through American FactFinder. About 2.9 percent of people reported more than one race in Census 2010.

[4] The "Outside metropolitan statistical areas" category includes both micropolitan statistical areas and territory outside of metropolitan and micropolitan statistical areas.

[5] The sum of those with and without a disability does not equal the total because disability status is not defined for individuals in the Armed Forces.

Source: U.S. Census Bureau, Current Population Survey, 2014 Annual Social and Economic Supplement.

Table 2.
People With Income Below Specified Ratios of Their Poverty Thresholds by Selected Characteristics: 2013

Numbers in thousands, confidence intervals [C.I.] in thousands or percentage points as appropriate. People as of March of the following year. For information on confidentiality protection, sampling error, nonsampling error, and definitions, see www.census.gov/prod/techdoc/cps/cpsmar14.pdf)

Income to Poverty Ratio	Traditional Income Questions					Redesigned Income Questions					Difference	
	Total	Number	90 percent C.I.[1] (+/-)	Percent	90 percent C.I.[1] (+/-)	Total	Number	90 percent C.I.[1] (+/-)	Percent	90 percent C.I.[1] (+/-)	Number	Percent
Under 50%												
All people............	312,970	19,870	587	6.35	0.2	313,100	19,914	964	6.36	0.3	44	0.0
Under age 18................	73,625	6,484	310	8.81	0.4	73,439	7,082	495	9.64	0.7 *	597 *	0.8
Aged 18 to 64................	194,830	12,165	391	6.24	0.2	194,690	11,530	607	5.92	0.3	-635	-0.3
Aged 65 and older.........	44,508	1,221	143	2.74	0.3	44,963	1,303	177	2.9	0.4	82	0.2
Below 125%												
All people............	312,970	60,215	1,129	19.24	0.4	313,100	60,159	1,508	19.21	0.5	-56	0.0
Under age 18................	73,625	19,215	473	26.1	0.6	73,439	19,634	770	26.73	1.1	419	0.6
Aged 18 to 64................	194,830	34,298	778	17.6	0.4	194,690	33,449	918	17.18	0.5	-849	-0.4
Aged 65 and older.........	44,508	6,702	284	15.06	0.6	44,963	7,077	369	15.74	0.8	375	0.7
Below 150%												
All people............	312,970	76,077	1,244	24.31	0.4	313,100	76,185	1,759	24.33	0.6	107	0.0
Under age 18................	73,625	23,656	502	32.13	0.7	73,439	24,260	822	33.03	1.1	604	0.9
Aged 18 to 64................	194,830	43,073	851	22.11	0.4	194,690	42,313	1,079	21.73	0.6	-760	-0.4
Aged 65 and older.........	44,508	9,348	327	21	0.7	44,963	9,612	438	21.38	1.0	264	0.4
Below 200%												
All people............	312,970	106,020	1,422	33.88	0.5	313,100	105,100	1,902	33.57	0.6	-923	-0.3
Under age 18................	73,625	31,364	538	42.6	0.7	73,439	31,772	796	43.26	1.1	408	0.7
Aged 18 to 64................	194,830	59,911	1,002	30.75	0.5	194,690	58,698	1,251	30.15	0.6	-1,213	-0.6
Aged 65 and older.........	44,508	14,749	386	33.14	0.9	44,963	14,630	510	32.54	1.1	-119	-0.6

*Significantly different from zero at the 90 percent confidence level.

[1] A 90 percent confidence interval is a measure of an estimate's variability. The larger the confidence interval in relation to the size of the estimate, the less reliable the estimate. Confidence intervals shown in this table are based on standard errors calculated using replicate weights instead of the generalized variance function used in the past. For more information see "Standard Errors and Their Use" at ftp://ftp2.census.gov/library/publications/2014/demo/p60-249sa.pdf.

Source: U.S. Census Bureau, Current Population Survey, 2014 Annual Social and Economic Supplement.

Table 3.
Income Deficit or Surplus of Families and Unrelated Individuals by Poverty Status: 2013

(Numbers of families and unrelated individuals in thousands, deficits and surpluses and their confidence intervals [C.I.] in dollars. For information on confidentiality protection, sampling error, nonsampling error, and definitions, see ftp://ftp2.census.gov/programs-surveys/cps/techdocs/cpsmar14.pdf)

| | Average Deficit or Surplus (dollars) | | | | | Deficit or Surplus Per Capita (dollars) | | | | | Median Deficit or Surplus (dollars) | | | | |
| | Traditional | | Redesigned | | Difference | Traditional | | Redesigned | | Difference | Traditional | | Redesigned | | Difference |
	Estimate	90 percent C.I.¹ (+/-)	Estimate	90 percent C.I.¹ (+/-)		Estimate	90 percent C.I.¹ (+/-)	Estimate	90 percent C.I.¹ (+/-)		Estimate	90 percent C.I.¹ (+/-)	Estimate	90 percent C.I.¹ (+/-)	
Below Poverty Threshold, Deficit															
All families	9,834	189	9,927	327	-93	2,848	66	2,923	102	-75	8,741	252	8,734	472	6
Married-couple families	9,013	309	9,148	578	-135	2,442	83	2,460	149	-18	7,625	431	6,961	827	664
Families with a female householder, no husband present	10,691	271	10,645	417	46	3,183	94	3,234	158	-51	9,816	401	9,634	519	182
Families with a male householder, no wife present	8,717	573	8,877	944	-160	2,841	219	3,101	358	-260	8,122	808	8,069	1,727	53
Unrelated individuals	6,422	154	6,308	194	114	6,422	154	6,308	194	114	5,861	455	5,661	496	200
Above Poverty Threshold, Surplus															
All families	74,667	1,161	78,468	1,611 *	-3,801	24,087	395	25,532	557 *	-1445	51,839	519	53,695	704 *	-1,856
Married-couple families	83,767	1,353	87,689	1,895 *	-3,923	26,600	444	28,102	641 *	-1502	57,315	451	58,907	585 *	-1,593
Families with a female householder, no husband present	37,245	1,254	41,545	3,513 *	-4,300	12,511	458	13,882	1,220 *	-1371	25,376	1,131	26,355	1,680	-979
Families with a male householder, no wife present	52,717	3,490	57,908	5,699	-5,191	18,668	1,254	21,050	2,137 *	-2382	33,805	1,518	38,163	3,823 *	-4,358
Unrelated individuals	34,066	819	35,849	1,285 *	-1,782	34,066	819	35,849	1,285 *	-1782	21,742	732	22,928	732 *	-1,185

*Significantly different from zero at the 90 percent confidence level.

¹A 90 percent confidence interval is a measure of an estimate's variability. The larger the confidence interval in relation to the size of the estimate, the less reliable the estimate. Confidence intervals shown in this table are based on standard errors calculated using replicate weights instead of the generalized variance function used in the past. For more information see "Standard Errors and Their Use" at ftp://ftp2.census.gov/library/publications/2014/demo/p60-249sa.pdf.

Note: Details may not sum to totals because of rounding.

Source: U.S. Census Bureau, Current Population Survey, 2014 Annual Social and Economic Supplement.

Table 4. Sample Composition Comparison 2013: Traditional vs. Redesigned Income Questions

(Numbers in thousands, confidence intervals (C.I.) in thousands or percentage points as appropriate. People as of March of the following year. For information on confidentiality protection, sampling error, nonsampling error, and definitions, see ftp://ftp2.census.gov/programs-surveys/cps/techdocs/cpsmar14.pdf)

Characteristics	Traditional Income Questions Number	90 Percent C.I. (+/-)	Percent	90 Percent C.I. (+/-)	Redesigned Income Questions Number	90 Percent C.I. (+/-)	Percent	90 Percent C.I. (+/-)	Redesigned minus Traditional Income Number	Percent
PEOPLE										
Total	312,970	124	100.0	0.0	313,100	200	100.0	0.0	131	0.0
Family Status										
In families	254,990	822	81.5	0.3	256,070	1,187	81.8	0.4	1,082	0.3
Householder	81,217	445	26.0	0.1	82,316	722	26.3	0.2 *	1,099 *	0.3
Related children under age 18	72,573	196	23.2	0.1	72,246	338	23.1	0.1	-327	-0.1
Related children under age 6	23,585	90	7.5	0.0	23,606	129	7.5	0.0	21	0.0
In unrelated subfamilies	1,413	153	0.5	0.0	1,626	298	0.5	0.1	213	0.1
Reference person	595	65	0.2	0.0	661	128	0.2	0.0	66	0.0
Children under age 18	714	84	0.2	0.0	844	167	0.3	0.1	130	0.0
Unrelated individual	56,564	826	18.1	0.3	55,400	1,156	17.7	0.4	-1,164	-0.4
Race[3] and Hispanic Origin										
White alone	243,080	202	77.7	0.1	243,350	305	77.7	0.1	262	0.1
White alone, not Hispanic	195,170	259	62.4	0.1	195,120	403	62.3	0.1	-50	0.0
Black alone	40,615	47	13.0	0.0	40,498	64	12.9	0.0 *	-117 *	0.0
Asian alone	17,063	305	5.5	0.1	17,257	392	5.5	0.1	194	0.1
Hispanic (of any race)	54,145	40	17.3	0.0	54,181	93	17.3	0.0	36	0.0
Sex										
Male	153,360	116	49.0	0.0	153,470	179	49.0	0.0	105	0.0
Female	159,600	46	51.0	0.0	159,630	77	51.0	0.0	26	0.0
Age										
Under age 18	73,625	184	23.5	0.1	73,439	285	23.5	0.1	-185	-0.1
Aged 18 to 64	194,830	216	62.3	0.1	194,690	465	62.2	0.1	-139	-0.1
Aged 65 and over	44,508	45	14.2	0.0	44,963	352	14.4	0.1 *	455 *	0.1
Nativity										
Native	271,970	728	86.9	0.2	272,420	1,068	87.0	0.3	454	0.1
Foreign born	40,997	716	13.1	0.2	40,673	1,000	13.0	0.3	-324	-0.1
Naturalized citizen	19,147	443	6.1	0.1	19,247	693	6.2	0.2	100	0.0
Not a citizen	21,850	592	7.0	0.2	21,426	849	6.8	0.3	-424	-0.1
Region										
Northeast	55,478	269	17.7	0.1	55,529	357	17.7	0.1	51	0.0
Midwest	66,785	222	21.3	0.1	66,732	342	21.3	0.1	-53	0.0
South	116,960	307	37.4	0.1	116,960	424	37.4	0.1	-5	0.0
West	73,742	228	23.6	0.1	73,879	383	23.6	0.1	137	0.0
Residence										
Inside metropolitan statistical areas	265,920	3,009	85.0	1.0	265,300	3,157	84.7	1.0	-615	-0.2
Inside principal cities	102,150	2,404	32.6	0.8	101,090	3,004	32.3	1.0	-1,055	-0.4

Table 4. Sample Composition Comparison 2013: Traditional vs. Redesigned Income Questions

(Numbers in thousands, confidence intervals (C.I.) in thousands or percentage points as appropriate. People as of March of the following year. For information on confidentiality protection, sampling error, nonsampling error, and definitions, see ftp://ftp2.census.gov/programs-surveys/cps/techdocs/cpsmar14.pdf)

Characteristics	Traditional Income Questions				Redesigned Income Questions				Redesigned minus Traditional Income	
	Number	90 Percent C.I. (+/-)	Percent	90 Percent C.I. (+/-)	Number	90 Percent C.I. (+/-)	Percent	90 Percent C.I. (+/-)	Number	Percent
Outside principal cities.	163,770	2,664	52.3	0.9	164,210	2,780	52.5	0.9	440	0.1
Outside metropolitan statistical areas[4]	47,050	2,992	15.0	1.0	47,795	3,181	15.3	1.0	745	0.2
Work Experience										
Total, aged 18 to 64	194,830	216	62.3	0.1	194,690	465	62.2	0.1	-139	-0.1
All workers (aged 18 to 64)	146,250	711	46.7	0.2	146,860	973	46.9	0.3	607	0.2
Worked full-time year-round	100,860	800	32.2	0.3	101,180	1,087	32.3	0.3	324	0.1
Not full-time year-round	45,397	638	14.5	0.2	45,680	860	14.6	0.3	283	0.1
Did not work at least one week	48,581	734	15.5	0.2	47,834	921	15.3	0.3	-746	-0.2
Disability Status[5]										
Total, aged 18 to 64	194,830	216	62.3	0.1	194,690	465	62.2	0.1	-139	-0.1
With a disability	15,098	441	4.8	0.1	14,461	612	4.6	0.2	-638	-0.2
Without a disability	178,760	445	57.1	0.1	179,210	676	57.2	0.2	445	0.1
People in Families										
Total in families	254,990	822	81.5	0.3	256,070	1,187	81.8	0.4	1,082	0.3
Married-couple..............	189,860	1,317	60.7	0.4	188,130	2,271	60.1	0.7	-1,728	-0.6
Female householder, no husband present.............	47,007	1,052	15.0	0.3	49,951	1,732	16.0	0.6 *	2,943 *	0.9
Male householder, no wife present	18,121	579	5.8	0.2	17,987	1,032	5.8	0.3	-134	0.0

*Significantly different from zero at the 90 percent confidence level.

[1] A 90 percent confidence interval is a measure of an estimate's variability. The larger the confidence interval in relation to the size of the estimate, the less reliable the estimate. Confidence intervals shown in this table are based on standard errors calculated using replicate weights instead of the generalized variance function used in the past. For more information see "Standard Errors and Their Use" at ftp://ftp2.census.gov/library/publications/2014/demo/p60-249sa.pdf.

[2] Details may not sum to totals because of rounding.

[3] Federal surveys now give respondents the option of reporting more than one race. Therefore, two basic ways of defining a race group are possible. A group such as Asian may be defined as those who reported Asian and no other race (the race-alone or single-race concept) or as those who reported Asian regardless of whether they also reported another race (the race-alone-or-in-combination concept). This table shows data using the first approach (race alone). The use of the single-race population does not imply that it is the preferred method of presenting or analyzing data. The Census Bureau uses a variety of approaches. Information on people who reported more than one race, such as White *and* American Indian and Alaska Native or Asian *and* Black or African American, is available from Census 2010 through American FactFinder. About 2.9 percent of people reported more than one race in Census 2010.

[4] The "Outside metropolitan statistical areas" category includes both micropolitan statistical areas and territory outside of metropolitan and micropolitan statistical areas.

[5] The sum of those with and without a disability does not equal the total because disability status is not defined for individuals in the Armed Forces.

Source: U.S. Census Bureau, Current Population Survey, 2014 Annual Social and Economic Supplements.

Table 5. Sample Composition Comparison 2013: Traditional vs. Redesign Income Questions - Persons Under Age 18

(Numbers in thousands, confidence intervals (C.I.) in thousands or percentage points as appropriate. People as of March of the following year. For information on confidentiality protection, sampling error, nonsampling error, and definitions, see ftp://ftp2.census.gov/programs-surveys/cps/techdocs/cpsmar14.pdf)

CHARACTERISTICS	Traditional Income Questions				Redesigned Income Questions				Difference: Redesigned minus Traditional	
	Number	90 Percent C.I. (+/-)	Percent	90 Percent C.I.	Number	90 Percent C.I. (+/-)	Percent	90 Percent C.I. (+/-)	Number	Percent
ALL CHILDREN UNDER AGE 18										
Total	73,625	184	100.0	0.0	73,439	285	100.0	0.0	-185	0.0
Family Status										
In families	72,772	197	98.8	0.1	72,409	333	98.6	0.2	-363	-0.2
Householder	193	41	0.3	0.1	162	61	0.2	0.1	-30	0
Related children under 18	72,573	196	98.6	0.1	72,246	338	98.4	0.3	-327	-0.2
Related children under 6	23,585	90	32.0	0.1	23,606	129	32.1	0.2	21	0.1
In unrelated subfamilies	714	84	1.0	0.1	844	167	1.2	0.2	130	0.2
Unrelated individual	139	33	0.2	0.0	187	64	0.3	0.1	48	0.1
Race[3] and Hispanic Origin										
White alone	53,846	163	73.1	0.1	53,638	244	73.0	0.2	-208	-0.1
White alone, not Hispanic	38,395	159	52.2	0.2	38,167	253	52.0	0.3	-228	-0.2
Black alone	11,088	77	15.1	0.1	11,003	118	15.0	0.1	-85	-0.1
Asian alone	3,651	108	5.0	0.1	3,766	172	5.1	0.2	115	0.2
Hispanic (of any race)	17,837	76	24.2	0.1	17,898	166	24.4	0.2	61	0.1
Sex										
Male	37,480	125	50.9	0.1	37,546	197	51.1	0.2	66	0.2
Female	36,144	138	49.1	0.1	35,893	206	48.9	0.2	* -251	-0.2
Nativity										
Native	70,925	237	96.3	0.2	71,092	378	96.8	0.4	* 166	0.5
Foreign born	2,700	159	3.7	0.2	2,348	266	3.2	0.4	* -352	-0.5
Naturalized citizen	778	88	1.1	0.1	765	144	1.0	0.2	-13	0
Not a citizen	1,922	136	2.6	0.2	1,583	202	2.2	0.3	* -338	-0.5
Region										
Northeast	11,983	112	16.3	0.1	12,105	181	16.5	0.2	122	0.2
Midwest	15,774	114	21.4	0.1	15,719	159	21.4	0.2	-54	0.0
South	28,036	151	38.1	0.2	27,773	225	37.8	0.3	-262	-0.3
West	17,832	110	24.2	0.1	17,841	165	24.3	0.2	9	0.1
Residence										

Table 5. Sample Composition Comparison 2013: Traditional vs. Redesign Income Questions - Persons Under Age 18

(Numbers in thousands, confidence intervals (C.I.) in thousands or percentage points as appropriate. People as of March of the following year. For information on confidentiality protection, sampling error, nonsampling error, and definitions, see ftp://ftp2.census.gov/programs-surveys/cps/techdocs/cpsmar14.pdf)

CHARACTERISTICS	Traditional Income Questions				Redesigned Income Questions				Difference: Redesigned minus Traditional	
	Number	90 Percent C.I. (+/-)	Percent	90 Percent C.I.	Number	90 Percent C.I. (+/-)	Percent	90 Percent C.I. (+/-)	Number	Percent
Inside metropolitan statistical areas......	62,859	792	85.4	1.0	62,526	944	85.1	1.2	-334	-0.2
Inside principal cities.............	24,108	720	32.7	1.0	23,647	912	32.2	1.2	-460	-0.5
Outside principal cities............	38,752	799	52.6	1.1	38,878	928	52.9	1.2	126	0.3
Outside metropolitan statistical areas[4] ...	10,765	743	14.6	1.0	10,914	876	14.9	1.2	148	0.2
People in Families										
Total	72,772	197	98.8	0.1	72,409	333	98.6	0.2	-363	-0.2
Married-couple.............	49,443	503	67.2	0.7	48,262	830	65.7	1.1	* -1,180	* -1.4
With related children under age 6	16,225	244	22.0	0.3	16,050	367	21.9	0.5	-176	-0.2
Female householder, no husband present.............	18,223	484	24.8	0.7	19,085	732	26.0	1	* 863	* 1.2
With related children under age 6	5,706	222	7.8	0.3	5,939	359	8.1	0.5	234	0.3
Male householder, no wife present.........	5,107	243	6.9	0.3	5,061	436	6.9	0.6	-45	0.0
With related children under age 6	1,655	121	2.3	0.2	1,617	218	2.2	0.3	-38	0.0

72772.0

*Significantly different from zero at the 90 percent confidence level.

[1] A 90 percent confidence interval is a measure of an estimate's variability. The larger the confidence interval in relation to the size of the estimate, the less reliable the estimate. Confidence intervals shown in this table are based on standard errors calculated using replicate weights instead of the generalized variance function used in the past. For more information see "Standard Errors and Their Use" at ftp://ftp2.census.gov/library/publications/2014/demo/p60-249sa.pdf.

[2] Details may not sum to totals because of rounding.

[3] Federal surveys now give respondents the option of reporting more than one race. Therefore, two basic ways of defining a race group are possible. A group such as Asian may be defined as those who reported Asian and no other race (the race-alone or single-race concept) or as those who reported Asian regardless of whether they also reported another race (the race-alone-or-in-combination concept). This table shows data using the first approach (race alone). The use of the single-race population does not imply that it is the preferred method of presenting or analyzing data. The Census Bureau uses a variety of approaches. Information on people who reported more than one race, such as White *and* American Indian and Alaska Native or Asian *and* Black or African American, is available from Census 2010 through American FactFinder. About 2.9 percent of people reported more than one race in Census 2010.

[4] The "Outside metropolitan statistical areas" category includes both micropolitan statistical areas and territory outside of metropolitan and micropolitan statistical areas.

Source: U.S. Census Bureau, Current Population Survey, 2014 Annual Social and Economic Supplements.

Table 6.
Children in Poverty by Selected Characteristics: 2013 Traditional Income Questions minus Redesign Income Questions

(Numbers in thousands, confidence intervals (C.I.) in thousands or percentage points as appropriate. People as of March of the following year. For information on confidentiality protection, sampling error, nonsampling error, and definitions, see ftp://ftp2.census.gov/programs-surveys/cps/techdocs/cpsmar14.pdf)

Characteristic	Total	Traditional Income Questions				Total	Redesigned Income Questions				Change in Poverty	
		Number in Poverty	90 C.I.[1] (+/-)	Percent in Poverty	90 C.I.[1] (+/-)		Number in Poverty	90 C.I.[1] (+/-)	Percent in Poverty	90 C.I.[1] (+/-)	Number	Percent
All Children	73,625	14,659	455	19.9	0.6	73,439	15,633	709	21.3	1.0	* 974	* 1.4
In families.............	72,772	14,190	447	19.5	0.6	72,409	15,047	705	20.8	1.0	* 858	* 1.3
Related children under 18.............	72,573	14,142	445	19.5	0.6	72,246	14,983	706	20.7	1.0	* 841	* 1.3
Related children under 6.............	23,585	5,231	225	22.2	1.0	23,606	5,495	338	23.3	1.4	264	1.1
In unrelated subfamilies.............	714	340	69	47.7	6.7	844	412	122	48.8	9.2	72	1.2
Unrelated individual.............	139	129	33	92.8	5.5	187	173	62	92.8	6.3	45	0.0
Race[3] and Hispanic Origin												
White alone.............	53,846	8,808	343	16.4	0.6	53,638	10,132	512	18.9	1.0	* 1,324	* 2.5
White alone, not Hispanic.............	38,395	4,094	255	10.7	0.7	38,167	5,007	381	13.1	1.0	* 913	* 2.5
Black alone.............	11,088	4,244	247	38.3	2.2	11,003	3,723	335	33.8	3.0	* -521	* -4.4
Asian alone.............	3,651	367	56	10.1	1.5	3,766	568	144	15.1	3.8	* 201	* 5.0
Hispanic (of any race).............	17,837	5,415	263	30.4	1.5	17,898	5,853	460	32.7	2.6	438	2.3
Sex												
Male.............	37,480	7,416	288	19.8	0.8	37,546	7,962	390	21.2	1.0	* 546	* 1.4
Female.............	36,144	7,242	257	20.0	0.7	35,893	7,670	426	21.4	1.2	428	* 1.3
Native.............	70,925	13,892	438	19.6	0.6	71,092	14,928	711	21.0	1.0	* 1,035	* 1.4
Foreign born.............	2,700	766	89	28.4	3.0	2,348	705	163	30.0	5.3	-61	1.6
Naturalized citizen.............	778	162	43	20.9	5.2	765	127	60	16.6	7.1	-35	-4.3
Not a citizen.............	1,922	604	77	31.4	3.6	1,583	578	144	36.5	6.9	-26	5.1
Region												
Northeast.............	11,983	2,099	188	17.5	1.6	12,105	2,183	306	18.0	2.5	85	0.5
Midwest.............	15,774	2,677	187	17.0	1.2	15,719	3,060	322	19.5	2.1	* 383	* 2.5
South.............	28,036	6,412	321	22.9	1.1	27,773	6,700	479	24.1	1.7	288	1.3
West.............	17,832	3,471	186	19.5	1.0	17,841	3,689	328	20.7	1.8	218	1.2

Table 6.
Children in Poverty by Selected Characteristics: 2013 Traditional Income Questions minus Redesign Income Questions

(Numbers in thousands, confidence intervals (C.I.) in thousands or percentage points as appropriate. People as of March of the following year. For information on confidentiality protection, sampling error, nonsampling error, and definitions, see ftp://ftp2.census.gov/programs-surveys/cps/techdocs/cpsmar14.pdf)

Characteristic	Total	Traditional Income Questions				Total	Redesigned Income Questions				Change in Poverty	
		Number in Poverty	90 percent C.I.[1] (+/-)	Percent in Poverty	90 percent C.I.[1] (+/-)		Number in Poverty	90 percent C.I.[1] (+/-)	Percent in Poverty	90 percent C.I.[1] (+/-)	Number	Percent
Residence												
Inside metropolitan statistical areas......	62,859	12,170	449	19.4	0.7	62,526	12,766	670	20.4	1.0	595	1.1
Inside principal cities..........	24,108	6,470	382	26.8	1.3	23,647	6,423	548	27.2	2.1	-47	0.3
Outside principal cities..........	38,752	5,700	313	14.7	0.7	38,878	6,343	463	16.3	1.1	* 642	1.6
Outside metropolitan statistical areas[4] ...	10,765	2,488	262	23.1	1.7	10,914	2,867	383	26.3	2.5	* 379	3.2
People Under Age 18 in Families												
Married-couple..........	49,443	4,700	285	9.5	0.6	48,262	4,844	459	10.0	0.9	144	0.5
Female householder, no husband present..........	18,223	8,339	362	45.8	1.5	19,085	8,963	597	47.0	2.1	624	1.2
Male householder, no wife present..........	5,107	1,151	129	22.5	2.2	5,061	1,240	224	24.5	3.9	89	2.0

*Significantly different from zero at the 90 percent confidence level.

[1]A 90 percent confidence interval is a measure of an estimate's variability. The larger the confidence interval in relation to the size of the estimate, the less reliable the estimate. Confidence intervals shown in this table are based on standard errors calculated using replicate weights instead of the generalized variance function used in the past. For more information see "Standard Errors and Their Use" at ftp://ftp2.census.gov/library/publications/2014/demo/p60-249sa.pdf.

[2]Details may not sum to totals because of rounding.

[3]Federal surveys now give respondents the option of reporting more than one race. Therefore, two basic ways of defining a race group are possible. A group such as Asian may be defined as those who reported Asian and no other race (the race-alone or single-race concept) or as those who reported Asian regardless of whether they also reported another race (the race-alone-or-in-combination concept). This table shows data using the first approach (race alone). The use of the single-race population does not imply that it is the preferred method of presenting or analyzing data. The Census Bureau uses a variety of approaches. Information on people who reported more than one race, such as White and American Indian and Alaska Native or Asian and Black or African American, is available from Census 2010 through American FactFinder. About 2.9 percent of people reported more than one race in Census 2010.

[4]The "Outside metropolitan statistical areas" category includes both micropolitan statistical areas and territory outside of metropolitan and micropolitan statistical areas.

Source: U.S. Census Bureau, Current Population Survey, 2014 Annual Social and Economic Supplement.

Table 7. Sample Composition Comparison 2013: Traditional vs. Redesigned Income Questions - People Aged 65 and Older

(Numbers in thousands, confidence intervals (C.I.) in thousands or percentage points as appropriate. People as of March of the following year. For information on confidentiality protection, sampling error, nonsampling error, and definitions, see ftp://ftp2.census.gov/programs-surveys/cps/techdocs/cpsmar14.pdf)

Characteristics	Traditional Income Questions				Redesigned Income Questions				Redesigned minus Traditional Income	
	Number	90 Percent C.I. (+/-)	Percent	90 Percent C.I. (+/-)	Number	90 Percent C.I. (+/-)	Percent	90 Percent C.I. (+/-)	Number	Percent
People Aged 65 and Older										
Total.........	44,508	45	100.0	0.0	44,963	352	100.0	0.0	* 455	0.0
Family Status										
In families.........	30,692	353	69.0	0.8	30,906	582	68.7	1.1	214	-0.2
Householder.........	15,608	288	35.1	0.6	15,731	446	35.0	0.9	123	-0.1
Unrelated individual.........	13,800	356	31.0	0.8	14,018	461	31.2	1.1	218	0.2
Male.........	4,389	186	9.9	0.4	4,581	315	10.2	0.7	192	0.3
Female.........	9,411	239	21.2	0.5	9,437	357	21.0	0.9	26	-0.2
Race[3] and Hispanic Origin										
White alone.........	37,905	78	85.2	0.2	38,475	365	85.6	0.3	* 570	* 0.4
White alone, not Hispanic.........	34,781	89	78.2	0.2	35,322	362	78.6	0.4	* 541	0.4
Black alone.........	3,975	44	8.9	0.1	3,933	16	8.8	0.1	-42	* -0.2
Asian alone.........	1,881	75	4.2	0.2	1,845	114	4.1	0.3	-36	-0.1
Hispanic (of any race).........	3,405	12	7.7	0.0	3,443	114	7.7	0.2	39	0.0
Sex										
Male.........	19,763	45	44.4	0.1	20,216	352	45.0	0.4	* 453	* 0.6
Female.........	24,745	0	55.6	0.1	24,747	2	55.0	0.4	2	* -0.6
Nativity										
Native.........	39,037	225	87.7	0.5	39,562	463	88.0	0.7	* 525	0.3
Foreign born.........	5,470	221	12.3	0.5	5,401	314	12.0	0.7	-69	-0.3
Naturalized citizen.........	4,037	200	9.1	0.5	4,018	308	8.9	0.7	-18	-0.1
Not a citizen.........	1,433	120	3.2	0.3	1,382	185	3.1	0.4	-51	-0.1
Region										
Northeast.........	8,269	258	18.6	0.6	8,492	358	18.9	0.8	223	0.3
Midwest.........	9,771	250	22.0	0.6	9,948	387	22.1	0.8	177	0.2
South.........	16,635	320	37.4	0.7	17,128	461	38.1	1.0	493	0.7
West.........	9,832	251	22.1	0.6	9,395	348	20.9	0.8	* -437	* -1.2

Table 7. Sample Composition Comparison 2013: Traditional vs. Redesigned Income Questions - People Aged 65 and Older

(Numbers in thousands, confidence intervals (C.I.) in thousands or percentage points as appropriate. People as of March of the following year. For information on confidentiality protection, sampling error, nonsampling error, and definitions, see ftp://ftp2.census.gov/programs-surveys/cps/techdocs/cpsmar14.pdf)

Characteristics	Traditional Income Questions				Redesigned Income Questions				Redesigned minus Traditional Income	
	Number	90 Percent C.I. (+/-)	Percent	90 Percent C.I. (+/-)	Number	90 Percent C.I. (+/-)	Percent	90 Percent C.I. (+/-)	Number	Percent
Residence										
Inside metropolitan statistical areas......	36,077	655	81.1	1.5	36,145	754	80.4	1.5	68	-0.7
Inside principal cities............	11,958	418	26.9	0.9	12,123	591	27.0	1.3	165	0.1
Outside principal cities............	24,119	615	54.2	1.4	24,022	757	53.4	1.6	-97	-0.8
Outside metropolitan statistical areas[4] ...	8,430	657	18.9	1.5	8,818	668	19.6	1.5	387	0.7
People in Families										
Total Aged 65 and Older in Families	30,692	353	69.0	0.8	30,906	582	68.7	1.1	214	-0.2
Married-couple.................	26,155	414	58.8	0.9	26,094	711	58.0	1.4	-61	-0.7
Female householder, no husband present..........	3,106	207	7.0	0.5	3,298	329	7.3	0.7	192	0.4
Male householder, no wife present.......	1,430	135	3.2	0.3	1,513	204	3.4	0.5	83	0.2

-Represents zero or rounds to zero.
*Significantly different from zero at the 90 percent confidence level.

[1]A 90 percent confidence interval is a measure of an estimate's variability. The larger the confidence interval in relation to the size of the estimate, the less reliable the estimate. Confidence intervals shown in this table are based on standard errors calculated using replicate weights instead of the generalized variance function used in the past. For more information see "Standard Errors and Their Use" at ftp://ftp2.census.gov/library/publications/2014/demo/p60-249sa.pdf.

[2]Details may not sum to totals because of rounding.

[3]Federal surveys now give respondents the option of reporting more than one race. Therefore, two basic ways of defining a race group are possible. A group such as

[4]The "Outside metropolitan statistical areas" category includes both micropolitan statistical areas and territory outside of metropolitan and micropolitan statistical areas.

[5]The sum of those with and without a disability does not equal the total because disability status is not defined for individuals in the Armed Forces.

Source: U.S. Census Bureau, Current Population Survey, 2014 Annual Social and Economic Supplements.

Table 8.
People Aged 65 and Older in Poverty by Selected Characteristics: 2013 Traditional Income Questions minus Redesigned Income Questions

(Numbers in thousands, confidence intervals (C.I.) in thousands or percentage points as appropriate. People as of March of the following year. For information on confidentiality protection, sampling error, nonsampling error, and definitions, see ftp://ftp2.census.gov/programs-surveys/cps/techdocs/cpsmar14.pdf)

Characteristic	Traditional Income Questions					Redesigned Income Questions					Change in Poverty	
	Total	Number in Poverty	90 percent C.I.[1] (+/-)	Percent in Poverty	90 percent C.I.[1] (+/-)	Total	Number in Poverty	90 percent C.I.[1] (+/-)	Percent in Poverty	90 percent C.I.[1] (+/-)	Number	Percent
People Aged 65 and Older												
Total...............	44,508	4,231	227	9.51	0.5	44,963	4,631	267	10.3	0.6	* 400	* 0.8
Family Status												
In families.................	30,692	1,819	161	5.9	0.5	30,906	1,731	217	5.6	0.7	-88	-0.3
Householder................	15,608	970	95	6.2	0.6	15,731	907	131	5.8	0.8	-62	-0.4
In unrelated subfamilies........	16	6	7	37.0	39.5	39	31	40	79.9	37.9	26	###
Reference person.............	2	2	3	100.0	0.0	24	20	23	83.5	32.5	18	###
Unrelated individual..........	13,800	2,406	167	17.4	1.1	14,018	2,869	226	20.5	1.4	* 463	* 3.0
Female...............	9,411	1,870	136	19.9	1.4	9,437	2,150	193	22.8	1.8	* 280	* 2.9
Male.................	4,389	536	71	12.2	1.5	4,581	719	130	15.7	2.6	* 183	* 3.5
Race[3] and Hispanic Origin												
White alone...........	37,905	3,197	205	8.4	0.5	38,475	3,403	233	8.8	0.6	206	0.4
White alone, not Hispanic...	34,781	2,569	191	7.4	0.6	35,322	2,804	227	7.9	0.6	235	0.6
Black alone...........	3,975	698	67	17.6	1.7	3,933	758	113	19.3	2.9	60	1.7
Asian alone...........	1,881	256	46	13.6	2.4	1,845	306	86	16.6	4.4	50	3.0
Hispanic (of any race).......	3,405	676	70	19.8	2.0	3,443	692	115	20.1	3.3	16	0.2
Sex												
Male..................	19,763	1,349	110	6.8	0.6	20,216	1,522	177	7.5	0.9	174	0.7
Female................	24,745	2,882	163	11.7	0.7	24,747	3,109	202	12.6	0.8	227	0.9
Nativity												
Native................	39,037	3,340	211	8.6	0.5	39,562	3,615	239	9.1	0.6	274	0.6
Foreign born...........	5,470	891	93	16.3	1.6	5,401	1,017	161	18.8	2.8	126	2.5
Naturalized citizen........	4,037	586	82	14.5	1.9	4,018	668	129	16.6	3.1	81	2.1
Not a citizen...........	1,433	304	63	21.2	3.8	1,382	349	97	25.2	6.1	45	4.0
Region												
Northeast.............	8,269	713	98	8.6	1.2	8,492	878	177	10.3	2.0	165	1.7
Midwest...............	9,771	725	95	7.4	1.0	9,948	847	112	8.5	1.1	122	1.1
South.................	16,635	1,826	163	11.0	1.0	17,128	1,776	198	10.4	1.1	-50	-0.6
West..................	9,832	967	91	9.8	0.9	9,395	1,131	162	12.0	1.7	* 163	* 2.2

Table 8.
People Aged 65 and Older in Poverty by Selected Characteristics: 2013 Traditional Income Questions minus Redesigned Income Questions

(Numbers in thousands, confidence intervals (C.I.) in thousands or percentage points as appropriate. People as of March of the following year. For information on confidentiality protection, sampling error, nonsampling error, and definitions, see ftp://ftp2.census.gov/programs-surveys/cps/techdocs/cpsmar14.pdf)

Characteristic	Traditional Income Questions					Redesigned Income Questions					Change in Poverty	
	Total	Number in Poverty	90 percent C.I.[1] (+/-)	Percent in Poverty	90 percent C.I.[1] (+/-)	Total	Number in Poverty	90 percent C.I.[1] (+/-)	Percent in Poverty	90 percent C.I.[1] (+/-)	Number	Percent
Residence												
Inside metropolitan statistical areas......	36,077	3,431	198	9.5	0.5	36,145	3,683	282	10.2	0.8	252	0.7
Inside principal cities..............	11,958	1,537	137	12.9	1.1	12,123	1,663	193	13.7	1.6	125	0.9
Outside principal cities.............	24,119	1,894	145	7.9	0.6	24,022	2,020	215	8.4	0.9	126	0.6
Outside metropolitan statistical areas[4]...	8,430	800	136	9.5	1.4	8,818	949	137	10.8	1.3	149	1.3
Family Kind												
Total in Families	30,692	1,819	161	5.9	0.5	30,906	1,731	217	5.6	0.7	-88	-0.3
Married-couple.................	26,155	1,203	149	4.6	0.6	26,094	1,115	196	4.3	0.7	-89	-0.3
Female householder, no husband present.................	3,106	426	68	13.7	2.0	3,298	455	95	13.8	2.8	29	0.1
Male householder, no wife present........	1,430	190	47	13.3	3.1	1,513	161	73	10.7	4.6	-28	-2.6

-Represents zero or rounds to zero.

*Significantly different from zero at the 90 percent confidence level.

[1]A 90 percent confidence interval is a measure of an estimate's variability. The larger the confidence interval in relation to the size of the estimate, the less reliable the estimate. Confidence intervals shown in this table are based on standard errors calculated using replicate weights instead of the generalized variance function used in the past. For more information see "Standard Errors and Their Use" at ftp://ftp2.census.gov/library/publications/2014/demo/p60-249sa.pdf.

[2]Details may not sum to totals because of rounding.

[3]Federal surveys now give respondents the option of reporting more than one race. Therefore, two basic ways of defining a race group are possible. A group such as Asian may be defined as those who reported Asian and no other race (the race-alone or single-race concept) or as those who reported Asian regardless of whether they also reported another race (the race-alone-or-in-combination concept). This table shows data using the first approach (race alone). The use of the single-race population does not imply that it is the preferred method of presenting or analyzing data. The Census Bureau uses a variety of approaches. Information on people who reported more than one race, such as White **and** American Indian and Alaska Native or Asian **and** Black or African American, is available from Census 2010 through American FactFinder. About 2.9 percent of people reported more than one race in Census 2010.

[4]The "Outside metropolitan statistical areas" category includes both micropolitan statistical areas and territory outside of metropolitan and micropolitan statistical areas.

Source: U.S. Census Bureau, Current Population Survey, 2014 Annual Social and Economic Supplement.

Table 9.
Number and Rate of Participation in Means-tested Programs: 2013 Redesigned Questions Minus Traditional Questions

(Numbers in thousands, confidence intervals (C.I.) in thousands or percentage points as appropriate. People as of March of the following year. For information on confidentiality protection, sampling error, nonsampling error, and definitions, see ftp://ftp2.census.gov/programs-surveys/cps/techdocs/cpsmar14.pdf)

Characteristics	Total	Traditional Income Questions			Redesigned Income Questions					Difference (Redesigned - Traditional)	
		Number	Percent	90 percent C.I.¹ (+/-)	Total	Number	90 percent C.I.¹ (+/-)	Percent	90 percent C.I.¹ (+/-)	Number	Percent
Home Energy Assistance Program											
All	312,970	9,411	3.0	0.2	313,100	9,847	690	3.2	0.2	437	0.1
Under 18 years	73,625	2,997	4.1	0.3	73,439	3,220	324	4.4	0.4	368	0.3
Aged 18 to 64	194,830	5,067	2.6	0.2	194,690	5,316	408	2.7	0.2	250	0.1
Aged 65 and older	44,508	1,347	3.0	0.3	44,963	1,311	183	2.9	0.4	(36)	-0.1
Medicaid											
All	312,970	53,786	17.2	0.4	313,100	55,832	1,452	17.8	0.5 *	2,046 *	0.6
Under 18 years	73,625	27,519	37.4	0.8	73,439	28,390	826	38.7	1.1	871	1.3
Aged 18 to 64	194,830	23,427	12.0	0.4	194,690	24,265	913	12.5	0.5	837	0.4
Aged 65 and older	44,508	2,840	6.4	0.4	44,963	3,177	286	7.1	0.6	338	0.7
SNAP											
All	312,970	38,446	12.3	0.4	313,100	42,947	1,413	13.7	0.5 *	4,502 *	1.4
Under 18 years	73,625	14,960	20.3	0.7	73,439	16,336	658	22.2	0.9 *	1,376 *	1.9
Aged 18 to 64	194,830	20,507	10.5	0.4	194,690	23,243	866	11.9	0.4 *	2,735 *	1.4
Aged 65 and older	44,508	2,978	6.7	0.4	44,963	3,368	279	7.5	0.6 *	390 *	0.8
Supplemental Security Income											
All	312,970	12,616	4.0	0.2	313,100	14,463	1,031	4.6	0.3 *	1,847 *	0.4
Under 18 years	73,625	2,502	3.4	0.3	73,439	3,344	431	4.6	0.6 *	842 *	0.6
Aged 18 to 64	194,830	8,223	4.2	0.2	194,690	8,914	674	4.6	0.3	691	0.4
Aged 65 and older	44,508	1,891	4.3	0.3	44,963	2,205	233	4.9	0.5 *	314 *	0.6

*Significantly different from zero at the 90 percent confidence level.

¹A 90 percent confidence interval is a measure of an estimate's variability. The larger the confidence interval in relation to the size of the estimate, the less reliable the estimate. Confidence intervals shown in this table are based on standard errors calculated using replicate weights instead of the generalized variance function used in the past. For more information see "Standard Errors and Their Use" at ftp://ftp2.census.gov/library/publications/2014/demo/p60-249sa.pdf.

Source: U.S. Census Bureau, Current Population Survey, 2014 Annual Social and Economic Supplement.

Table 10. Changes in Specific Income Sources for People with Household Income in the Lowest Quintile: 2013

Restricted to all households at or below the 20th percentile.

(Numbers in thousands, confidence intervals (C.I.) in thousands or percentage points as appropriate. People as of March of the following year. For information on confidentiality protection, sampling error, nonsampling error, and definitions, see ftp://ftp2.census.gov/programs-surveys/cps/techdocs/cpsmar14.pdf)

TYPE OF INCOME	Traditional Income Questions				Redesigned Income Questions				Percentage change in Number [3/8 - 5/8/5/8]		Percentage change in Aggregate Income [3/8 - 5/8/5/8]	
	Number		Aggregate income dollars		Number		Aggregate income dollars		Percentage change in Number with income [(3/8-5/8)/5/8]	Standard error of change in Number with income [(3/8-5/8)/5/8]	Percentage change in Aggregate income with income [(3/8-5/8)/5/8]	Standard error of change in Aggregate Income with income [(3/8-5/8)/5/8]
	Estimate	SE	Estimate	SE	Estimate	SE	Estimate	SE				
Earning from longest job.	10,905		101,392,562	2,198,795	10,371	295	94,638,544	3,122,310	-4.90	3.02 *	-6.66	3.49
Wages and Salary	9,831	216	94,504,592	2,242,149	9,358	287	88,238,468	2,992,782	-4.80	3.22 *	-6.63	3.64
Nonfarm Self-Employment	1,032	65	6,564,726	527,532	942	89	6,324,869	890,370	-8.78	10.38	-3.65	15.28
Farm Self-Employment	42	11	323,243	130,552	70	22	75,207	178,752	68.80	71.11	-76.73	61.56
Unemployment Compensation	1,010	61	5,231,591	413,029	811	90	4,656,736	608,217 *	-19.66	10.41 *	-10.99	13.98
Workers' Compensation	132	23	720,470	156,406	80	28	455,055	213,391 *	-39.26	23.50 *	-36.84	33.85
Social Security	11,220	212	122,891,903	2,403,285	10,979	296	120,735,773	3,398,084	-2.15	3.01	-1.75	3.20
SSI (Supplemental Security)	3,075	128	21,732,880	966,298	3,024	158	21,160,426	1,298,086	-1.66	6.64	-2.63	7.24
Public Assistance	977	62	2,979,305	254,926	1,159	101	4,032,816	407,512	18.58	12.41 *	35.36	17.56
Veterans' Benefits	334	38	2,454,080	321,323	365	43	1,856,469	315,617	9.28	18.05	-24.35	15.94
Survivors' Benefits	515	50	2,504,098	304,926	455	57	2,081,730	331,776	-11.61	13.47	-16.87	16.80
Disability Benefits	290	31	2,002,804	246,806	495	60	3,440,811	501,868 *	70.89	25.23 *	71.80	29.10
Pension Income	1,387	72	6,400,944	428,818	1,591	136	5,902,932	781,937	14.65	11.16	-7.78	14.02
Company or Union Retirement	1,017	66	3,861,444	334,562	743	83	3,136,188	600,315 *	-26.88	9.23 *	-18.78	17.74
Federal Government Retirement	69	14	592,550	159,682	32	15	137,135	78,017 *	-53.48	24.08 *	-76.86	15.26
IRA, KEOGH, OR 401(K)	38	13	188,346	109,468	267	47	932,924	229,655 *	611.23	321.61 *	395.33	430.28
Annuities	15	10	15,975	10,018	215	43	760,194	277,699	1304.06	1262.30 *	4658.76	4347.47
Interest.	5,526	152	2,501,775	206,354	7,726	289	2,579,337	296,396 *	39.80	6.56 *	3.10	14.51
Dividends	958	62	1,301,070	156,511	1,452	120	1,868,474	296,981 *	51.51	18.00 *	43.61	32.06

*Significantly different from zero at the 90 percent confidence level.

[1] A 90 percent confidence interval is a measure of an estimate's variability. The larger the confidence interval in relation to the size of the estimate, the less reliable the estimate. Confidence interval errors calculated using replicate weights instead of the generalized variance function used in the past. For more information see "Standard Errors and Their Use" at ftp://ftp2.census.gov/library/pub

Source: U.S. Census Bureau, Current Population Survey, 2014 Annual Social and Economic Supplement.

Appendix Table A. Comparing Aggregate Income, Mean Income and Recipiency Rates for Families with Children below 200% of the Poverty Threshold: Traditional vs Redesigned Income Questions: 2013

(Numbers in thousands, confidence intervals (C.I.) in thousands or percentage points as appropriate. People as of March of the following year. For information on confidentiality protection, sampling error, nonsampling error, and definitions, see ftp://ftp2.census.gov/programs-surveys/cps/techdocs/cpsmar14.pdf)

	AGGREGATE (in millions)						MEAN (for those with a positive report)						RECIPIENCY RATE					
	Traditional		Redesigned				Traditional		Redesigned				Traditional		Redesigned			
	Estimate	SE	Estimate	SE	Z-Score	Sig?	Estimate	SE	Estimate	SE	Z-Score	Sig?	Estimate	SE	Estimate	SE	Z-Score	Sig?
All Families with Children below 200% of poverty																		
Hours Worked	115,415	1,953	114,690	2,321	0.239	No	2,313	20	2,263	27	1.494	No	84.3%	0.5%	83.6%	0.7%	0.880	No
Social Security	97,393	5,086	103,955	7,016	0.757	No	14,064	366	12,855	371	2.318	Yes	11.7%	0.5%	13.3%	0.7%	1.826	Yes
SSI	35,553	2,126	45,937	4,637	2.036	Yes	8,855	251	8,769	577	0.136	No	6.8%	0.3%	8.6%	0.7%	2.430	Yes
Retirement Income	13,748	2,591	7,776	1,650	1.944	Yes	12,877	1,439	8,867	1,385	2.008	Yes	1.8%	0.2%	1.4%	0.2%	1.150	No
Disability Income	4,244	592	12,155	2,371	3.237	Yes	8,116	771	9,597	1,083	1.114	No	0.9%	0.1%	2.1%	0.3%	3.750	Yes
Interest	3,075	390	8,630	1,377	3.882	Yes	345	41	491	75	1.714	Yes	15.1%	0.5%	29.0%	1.0%	12.273	Yes
Earnings	1,347,827	22,943	1,328,199	29,718	0.523	No	27,063	258	26,265	380	1.735	Yes	84.2%	0.5%	83.4%	0.7%	0.933	No
Dividend Income	2,526	449	2,155	939	0.357	No	1,575	237	1,391	526	0.317	No	2.7%	0.2%	2.6%	0.4%	0.370	No
Survivors Income	2,702	653	2,221	738	0.487	No	7,378	1,152	4,473	932	1.960	Yes	0.6%	0.1%	0.8%	0.2%	0.763	No
Public Assistance	15,508	1,012	20,810	2,029	2.338	Yes	3,863	166	4,200	290	1.006	No	6.8%	0.3%	8.2%	0.6%	2.023	Yes
Food Stamps	105,784	2,768	111,017	4,011	1.074	No	4,287	60	4,180	101	0.911	No	41.7%	0.7%	43.8%	1.0%	1.681	Yes
Total Income	1,627,558	25,458	1,639,895	33,679	0.292	No	28,804	243	28,307	353	1.159	No	95.5%	0.3%	95.5%	0.4%	0.080	No
White, Asian, Other and Two or More Races																		
Hours Worked	95,933	1,737	94,851	2,381	0.367	No	2,395	22	2,308	32	2.230	Yes	86.2%	0.5%	85.4%	0.8%	0.939	No
Social Security	76,735	4,444	78,556	6,399	0.234	No	14,597	372	12,793	456	3.066	Yes	11.3%	0.6%	12.8%	0.8%	1.448	No
SSI	23,366	1,775	29,978	3,987	1.515	No	8,957	323	8,420	702	0.695	No	5.6%	0.4%	7.4%	0.7%	2.181	Yes
Retirement Income	8,965	1,650	4,111	1,169	2.400	Yes	12,209	1,226	7,755	1,886	1.980	Yes	1.6%	0.2%	1.1%	0.2%	1.580	No
Disability Income	3,633	560	9,974	2,099	2.919	Yes	8,363	854	10,699	1,209	1.578	No	0.9%	0.1%	1.9%	0.3%	2.903	Yes
Interest	2,831	385	7,422	1,273	3.453	Yes	364	47	514	84	1.562	No	16.7%	0.6%	30.0%	1.1%	10.828	Yes
Earnings	1,132,887	20,583	1,104,118	29,819	0.794	No	28,346	300	26,947	425	2.689	Yes	86.0%	0.5%	85.1%	0.8%	1.006	No
Dividend Income	1,921	356	2,134	938	0.212	No	1,408	225	1,448	557	0.068	No	2.9%	0.3%	3.1%	0.4%	0.239	No
Survivors Income	1,977	518	1,703	641	0.332	No	6,547	1,086	4,004	951	1.761	Yes	0.7%	0.1%	0.9%	0.3%	0.790	No
Public Assistance	8,927	776	14,843	1,892	2.893	Yes	3,559	191	4,473	387	2.121	Yes	5.4%	0.3%	6.9%	0.6%	2.082	Yes
Food Stamps	71,160	2,365	78,573	3,400	1.790	Yes	4,139	72	4,023	112	0.874	No	37.0%	0.8%	40.6%	1.2%	2.500	Yes
Total Income	1,344,868	22,774	1,339,080	33,663	0.142	No	30,259	282	29,050	402	2.464	Yes	95.7%	0.3%	95.8%	0.4%	0.162	No
Black Alone																		
Hours Worked	19,483	742	19,839	876	0.310	No	1,981	42	2,067	55	1.253	No	77.4%	1.3%	76.8%	1.7%	0.288	No
Social Security	20,658	2,210	25,399	3,075	1.252	No	12,385	857	13,053	705	0.602	No	13.1%	1.0%	15.6%	1.7%	1.253	No
SSI	12,187	1,255	15,959	2,535	1.334	No	8,665	387	9,510	965	0.813	No	11.1%	1.0%	13.4%	1.6%	1.241	No
Retirement Income	4,783	1,944	3,665	1,086	0.502	No	14,348	3,767	10,567	1,982	0.888	No	2.6%	0.6%	2.8%	0.7%	0.167	No
Disability Income	611	212	2,182	740	2.040	Yes	6,903	2,080	6,525	1,560	0.146	No	0.7%	0.2%	2.7%	0.7%	2.677	Yes
Interest	244	61	1,209	420	2.270	Yes	213	50	385	128	1.250	No	9.0%	1.0%	25.1%	2.0%	7.164	Yes
Earnings	214,940	8,275	224,081	10,934	0.667	No	21,850	488	23,351	747	1.682	Yes	77.4%	1.3%	76.8%	1.7%	0.288	No
Dividend Income	605	241	21	8	2.425	Yes	2,525	795	281	118	2.790	Yes	1.9%	0.5%	0.6%	0.2%	2.428	Yes
Survivors Income	724	352	518	313	0.438	No	11,295	3,584	7,272	2,239	0.952	No	0.5%	0.2%	0.6%	0.3%	0.193	No
Public Assistance	6,581	708	5,968	782	0.581	No	4,371	290	3,645	266	1.844	Yes	11.8%	0.9%	13.1%	1.6%	0.695	No
Food Stamps	34,623	1,596	32,444	2,340	0.769	No	4,627	117	4,619	216	0.033	No	58.9%	1.7%	56.2%	2.2%	0.955	No
Total Income	282,690	9,761	300,815	12,356	1.151	No	23,441	524	25,414	737	2.180	Yes	94.9%	0.7%	94.7%	0.9%	0.142	No
Asian																		
Hours Worked	6,233	482	6,077	614	0.201	No	2,715	105	2,580	123	0.834	No	88.8%	1.8%	87.1%	3.4%	0.422	No
Social Security	4,567	1,072	3,839	1,107	0.472	No	15,710	1,759	10,184	1,122	2.649	Yes	11.2%	2.5%	13.9%	3.6%	0.614	No
SSI	647	291	2,551	1,166	1.584	No	7,383	1,111	13,180	1,339	3.332	Yes	3.4%	1.4%	7.2%	3.1%	1.122	No
Retirement Income	85	68	392	373	0.811	No	9,481	2,107	20,623	9,362	1.161	No	0.3%	0.3%	0.7%	0.5%	0.617	No
Disability Income	12	13	107	101	0.933	No	8,400	-	2,521	1,551	3.791	Yes	0.1%	0.1%	1.6%	1.1%	1.393	No
Interest	88	23	219	67	1.852	Yes	140	34	203	58	0.938	No	24.4%	3.0%	40.0%	4.5%	2.843	Yes
Earnings	73,613	5,780	70,589	7,296	0.325	No	32,105	1,131	29,968	1,563	1.108	No	88.6%	1.8%	87.1%	3.4%	0.393	No
Dividend Income	236	152	17	11	1.436	No	1,932	1,102	406	294	1.339	No	4.7%	1.3%	1.6%	1.1%	1.869	Yes
Survivors Income	35	26	52	49	0.293	No	6,456	458	2,184	196	8.578	Yes	0.2%	0.2%	0.9%	0.8%	0.816	No
Public Assistance	764	308	1,353	481	1.030	No	4,617	766	6,871	1,614	1.262	No	6.4%	2.1%	7.3%	2.1%	0.301	No
Food Stamps	3,008	588	3,308	688	0.332	No	4,733	597	4,177	554	0.682	No	24.6%	2.8%	29.3%	4.7%	0.866	No
Total Income	84,368	6,410	85,075	8,318	0.067	No	33,618	1,275	32,871	1,587	0.367	No	97.0%	1.2%	95.7%	1.6%	0.648	No

*Significantly different from zero at the 90 percent confidence level.

[1] A 90 percent confidence interval is a measure of an estimate's variability. The larger the confidence interval in relation to the size of the estimate, the less reliable the estimate. Confidence intervals shown in this table are based on standard errors calculated using replicate weights instead of the generalized variance function used in the past. For more information see "Standard Errors and Their Use" at ftp://ftp2.census.gov/library/publications/2014/demo/p60-249sa.pdf.

Source: U.S. Census Bureau, Current Population Survey, 2014 Annual Social and Economic Supplement.

Appendix Table B. Comparing Aggregate Income, Mean Income and Recipiency Rates for Persons Aged 65 or Older with Income Below 200 Percent of Poverty: Traditional Income Questions vs. Redesigned Income Questions: 2013

(Numbers in thousands, confidence intervals (C.I.) in thousands or percentage points as appropriate. People as of March of the following year. For information on confidentiality protection, sampling error, nonsampling error, and definitions, see ftp://ftp2.census.gov/programs-surveys/cps/techdocs/cpsmar14.pdf)

| | AGGREGATE (in millions) | | | | | | MEAN (for those with a positive report) | | | | | | RECIPIENCY RATE | | | | | |
| | Traditional | | Redesigned | | | | Traditional | | Redesigned | | | | Traditional | | Redesigned | | | |
	Estimate	SE	Estimate	SE	Z-Score	Sig?	Estimate	SE	Estimate	SE	Z-Score	Sig?	Estimate	SE	Estimate	SE	Z-Score	Sig?
Unrelated Individuals and One Person Families																		
Hours Worked	1,661	96	1,842	171	0.923	No	1,321	45	1,349	83	0 305172	No	11.2%	0.6%	12.1%	0.9%	0.863912	No
Social Security	137,361	2,515	134,809	3,708	0.569	No	14,127	112	13,943	157	0.955	No	86.3%	0.6%	85.7%	1.0%	0.502	No
SSI	6,402	510	6,641	701	0.275	No	7,278	319	6,057	397	2.394	Yes	7.8%	0.5%	9.7%	0.7%	2.195	Yes
Retirement Income	8,507	544	7,792	801	0.738	No	5,175	255	5,098	400	0.163	No	14.6%	0.7%	13.5%	0.8%	0.952	No
Disability Income	287	87	864	341	1.642	No	7,085	1,145	8,187	1,567	0.567	No	0.4%	0.1%	0.9%	0.3%	1.908	Yes
Interest	2,366	199	2,071	271	0.877	No	680	55	455	59	2.790	Yes	30.9%	0.9%	40.4%	1.3%	6.044	Yes
Earnings	14,971	884	15,299	1,615	0.178	No	12,067	442	11,473	780	0.663	No	11.0%	0.6%	11.8%	0.9%	0.761	No
Dividend Income	938	113	1,148	210	0.880	No	1,376	144	1,154	189	0.935	No	6.0%	0.4%	8.8%	0.7%	3.255	Yes
Survivors Income	2,099	284	2,529	474	0.778	No	4,925	425	4,951	583	0.035	No	3.8%	0.4%	4.5%	0.6%	0.984	No
Public Assistance	205	60	292	72	0.927	No	2,712	569	2,191	421	0.737	No	0.7%	0.1%	1.2%	0.2%	1.823	Yes
Food Stamps	3,151	190	3,382	327	0.610	No	1,657	79	1,614	103	0.336	No	16.9%	0.7%	18.6%	1.1%	1.317	No
Total Income	177,092	3,096	175,895	4,530	0.218	No	16,221	134	16,090	202	0.540	No	96.9%	0.3%	96.9%	0.5%	0.031	No
Living in the West																		
Hours Worked	1,027	110	1,050	131	0.131	No	1,955	138	1,747	129	1.096168	No	16.7%	1.3%	19.2%	2.2%	0.966957	No
Social Security	37,619	1,629	34,605	2,452	1.024	No	15,036	278	13,958	420	2.138	Yes	79.5%	1.5%	79.2%	2.5%	0.102	No
SSI	3,546	564	2,759	555	0.994	No	10,188	897	6,656	812	2.919	Yes	11.1%	1.2%	13.2%	1.9%	0.963	No
Retirement Income	2,041	302	2,619	691	0.767	No	6,568	691	6,478	1,108	0.069	No	9.9%	1.0%	12.9%	1.9%	1.401	No
Disability Income	116	52	283	161	0.991	No	7,514	1,103	5,583	2,512	0.704	No	0.5%	0.2%	1.6%	0.9%	1.195	No
Interest	676	131	514	151	0.810	No	804	140	402	114	2.229	Yes	26.7%	1.6%	40.8%	2.7%	4.538	Yes
Earnings	9,777	1,091	10,518	1,278	0.441	No	18,955	1,369	17,505	1,631	0.681	No	16.4%	1.3%	19.2%	2.2%	1.087	No
Dividend Income	245	53	310	105	0.556	No	1,338	218	1,336	326	0.005	No	5.8%	1.0%	7.4%	1.7%	0.835	No
Survivors Income	324	113	413	114	0.555	No	5,098	1,325	3,964	868	0.716	No	2.0%	0.5%	3.3%	0.8%	1.468	No
Public Assistance	130	51	283	130	1.096	No	3,367	908	4,262	1,167	0.605	No	1.2%	0.4%	2.1%	0.8%	1.077	No
Food Stamps	823	105	808	152	0.078	No	1,841	151	2,092	216	0.950	No	14.2%	1.6%	12.3%	1.8%	0.764	No
Total Income	56,124	2,170	53,832	3,245	0.587	No	18,624	392	17,784	486	1.346	No	95.7%	0.8%	96.7%	1.1%	0.704	No

*Significantly different from zero at the 90 percent confidence level.

[1] A 90 percent confidence interval is a measure of an estimate's variability. The larger the confidence interval in relation to the size of the estimate, the less reliable the estimate. Confidence intervals shown in this table are based on standard errors calculated using replicate weights instead of the generalized variance function used in the past. For more information see "Standard Errors and Their Use" at ftp://ftp2.census.gov/library/publications/2014/demo/p60-249sa.pdf.

Source: U.S. Census Bureau, Current Population Survey, 2014 Annual Social and Economic Supplement.